FIRST
PEOPLES
of NORTH
AMERICA

THE PEOPLE AND CULTURE OF THE
WAMPANOAG

CASSIE M. LAWTON
RAYMOND BIAL

Cavendish
Square

New York

Published in 2017 by Cavendish Square Publishing, LLC
243 5th Avenue, Suite 136, New York, NY 10016

Copyright © 2017 by Cavendish Square Publishing, LLC

First Edition

Website: cavendishsq.com

This publication represents the opinions and views of the author based on his or her personal experience, knowledge, and research. The information in this book serves as a general guide only. The author and publisher have used their best efforts in preparing this book and disclaim liability rising directly or indirectly from the use and application of this book.

CPSIA Compliance Information: Batch #CS16CSQ

All websites were available and accurate when this book was sent to press.

Library of Congress Cataloging-in-Publication Data

Names: Lawton, Cassie M., author. | Bial, Raymond, author.
Title: The people and culture of the Wampanoag / Cassie M. Lawton and Raymond Bial.
Description: New York : Cavendish Square Publishing, 2016. | Series: First Peoples of North America |
Includes bibliographical references and index. | Description based on print version record and CIP data provided by publisher; resource not viewed. Identifiers: LCCN 2016000363 (print) | LCCN 2015051338 (ebook) |
ISBN 9781502618993 (ebook) | ISBN 9781502618986 (library bound) Subjects: LCSH: Wampanoag Indians--History--Juvenile literature. | Wampanoag Indians--Social life and customs--Juvenile literature. Classification:
LCC E99.W2 (print) | LCC E99.W2 L39 2016 (ebook) | DDC 974.4004/97348--dc23
LC record available at http://lccn.loc.gov/2016000363

Editorial Director: David McNamara
Editor: Kristen Susienka
Copy Editor: Rebecca Rohan
Art Director: Jeffrey Talbot
Designer: Amy Greenan
Production Assistant: Karol Szymczuk
Photo Research: J8 Media

Printed in the United States of America

ACKNOWLEDGMENTS

We would like to thank everyone involved in this project, especially Cavendish Square Publishing for their dedication to publishing this book. As always, we would like to thank our families for their constant support of our work.

CONTENTS

A Wampanoag woman wears a deerskin robe.

AUTHORS' NOTE

At the dawn of the twentieth century, Native Americans were thought to be a vanishing race. However, despite four hundred years of warfare, deprivation, and disease, Native Americans have persevered. Countless thousands have lost their lives, but over the course of this century and the last, the populations of Native tribes have grown tremendously. Even as America's First Peoples struggle to adapt to modern Western life, they have also kept the flame of their traditions alive—the languages, religions, stories, and the everyday ways of life. An exhilarating renaissance in Native American culture is now sweeping the continent from coast to coast.

The First Peoples of North America books depict the social and cultural life of the major nations, from the early history of Native peoples in North America to their present-day struggles for survival and dignity. Historical and contemporary photographs of traditional subjects, as well as period illustrations, are blended throughout each book so that readers may gain a sense of family life in a tipi, a hogan, or a longhouse.

No single book can comprehensively portray the intricate and varied lifeways of an entire tribe, or nation. We only hope that young people will come away with a deeper appreciation for the rich tapestry of Native American culture—both then and now—and a keen desire to learn more about these first Americans.

The shores of Massachusetts offered food and solace for many Wampanoag people.

CHAPTER ONE

The Wampanoag first lived in Massachusetts and Rhode Island.

A CULTURE BEGINS

There are many stories about the arrival of the first people in North America. Most accounts tell of the first humans migrating from Asia around ten thousand years ago by way of a land bridge over the Bering Strait. In the generations that followed, men, women, and children wandered the vast continent, forming family groups and later larger communities. These were the first people of the region. Today their descendants are called Native Americans. One of the groups to come from the first human populations in North America was the **Wampanoag** (wam-pu-NO-ug).

The Wampanoag Begin

The name Wampanoag is probably derived from *Wapanacki*, which means "people of the east" or "people of the dawn." For countless generations, the Wampanoag made their home in what are now the states of **Massachusetts** and Rhode Island. As early as 2270 BCE, people were hunting and fishing on Martha's Vineyard. People were settling on the island by 1380 CE. Over time, the Wampanoag adapted to living in the woods and on the water and learned to provide for themselves. The men built circular houses, hunted, traded for various goods, and fought with neighboring peoples. Women managed their households, took care of children, planted crops, gathered wild berries, caught shellfish, and made clothing, mats, and baskets.

Originally, this region was dotted with forests, rivers, lakes, marshes, and coastal waters. It was a rocky landscape once scoured by glaciers, yet temperate enough that people could grow corn, beans, and squash in clearings around their villages or along the coast. Winters could be brutally cold, with heavy snowfalls, yet the summer growing season was relatively long. The soil was not particularly fertile, but generations of tree leaves had decayed on the forest floor, creating a layer that covered the bedrock.

Amid the wilderness, there were extensive patches of cleared land. In these clearings, the Wampanoag

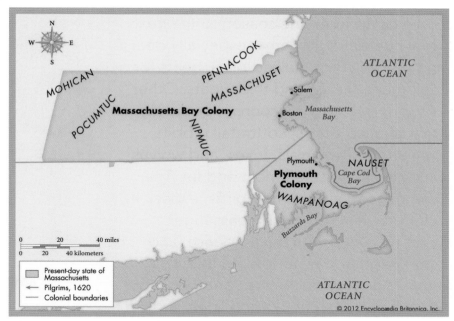

This map shows the area of Massachusetts the Wampanoag tribes eventually called home.

built wigwams and tended crops. Every spring and fall, the Wampanoag set fire to the underbrush in the forests around their villages. The ashes helped to fertilize the soil. Towering trees remained in an open forest, and sunlight penetrated to the ground, encouraging the growth of new plants. This careful burning improved hunting and gathering. Deer could forage on the tender, young shoots, and game had less cover. Hunters could move easily through the forest, and women could gather the wild blueberries that flourished on the burned areas.

For generations, the Wampanoag routinely managed the woods, making seasonal rounds to hunt, fish, gather, and trade with other peoples. They would set up their villages in one area for summer and would move camp from one season to the next. They hunted large game, especially deer and moose. They stalked black bears for their meat and fat and thick coats. Other animals, including raccoons, opossums, woodchucks, otters, cottontail rabbits, gray and red squirrels, foxes, and wolves were caught for their meat and fur. The Wampanoag also hunted birds, especially wild turkeys, grouse, and passenger pigeons, along with ducks, geese, and other migrating waterfowl. In the clear streams and lakes, they caught fish with spears, nets, and hooks and lines. To trap eels and fish swimming upriver to spawn, they built **weirs** of stones interlaced with branches. These migrating fish included suckers, sturgeon, shad, pickerel, and walleyed pike.

Over time, the Wampanoag shifted their seasonal migrations to partake of the bounty of fish and shellfish in the coastal waters. Once a year, they moved to the ocean to dig oysters and **quahogs** in the shallow water and to catch saltwater fish, such as alewives or the occasional swordfish. They also trapped lobsters and crabs for their succulent meat. It is likely that the Wampanoag also snatched seabirds from their nests and caught sea mammals, including seals, porpoises, and whales.

Dolphins and porpoises are common sights in the waters around Cape Cod.

Storytellers

In addition to their ways of everyday living, the Wampanoag passed down their history and traditions. This was done through storytelling. In the evenings, the young and old gathered around the fire to listen to the elders recount the tribe's origins. These tales allowed people to gain a better understanding of their place in the universe. Many of the stories of the Wampanoag of **Aquinnah** on Martha's Vineyard center on a benevolent giant named **Moshup**. Helen Manning, a Wampanoag elder born on Martha's Vineyard, recalled her grandmother telling her that Moshup was "taller than the tallest tree and as large around as the spread of a full-grown pine." Here is a story about how Moshup created the island of **Noepe**:

Many years ago, Noepe, or Martha's Vineyard, was not an island. It was part of the seventy-mile Cape Cod peninsula that curves gracefully into the Atlantic Ocean. When Moshup was a boy, he accompanied his father on hunting and fishing trips along the coast. Both father and son towered over the tallest trees. From that height, they could gaze over all the lands of the Wampanoag in Massachusetts and Rhode Island. Moshup glanced over the coastal plain and told his father that he was magically drawn to Noepe and wished to settle there.

Moshup was not happy on the mainland. However, everything appeared to be perfect in Noepe, except that no one lived there. One day, Moshup called his many cousins together. He told them of the beauty of Noepe and the abundance of fish in the seas and game in the forests. Moshup decided to make a new home on Noepe, and he invited his cousins to accompany him.

Once on Noepe, Moshup and his cousins wandered through the shadowy forest. They waded across bogs and marshes and trudged over sand dunes. Weary from his long journey, Moshup began to drag his heavy feet, leaving a track into which a little water trickled. It was just a silver thread, but the ocean winds, the rolling waves, and the tides quickly deepened and widened the channel. In rushed the waters of the sea to separate Noepe from the mainland.

Moshup's cousins and their families settled at various places on the island. They established small villages, each of which was governed by a **sachem** and a council of elders. Known as sachemships, these settlements included Taakemmy, meaning "mid-island place to grind corn"; Nunne-peg, or "the water people"; and Chappaquiddick, or "separate island." Pleased that his cousins had established a peaceful and prosperous society, Moshup founded his own sachemship at Aquinnah Cliffs. He lived there with his wife Squant and their many children in a place known as Moshup's Den. He taught his cousins how to catch fish, clams, and sea mammals and, over the ages, helped them to prosper in

This etching shows Pilgrim Edward Winslow meeting Massasoit.

The People and Culture of the Wampanoag

many other ways. To this day, in the spirit of Moshup, the Wampanoag care for the island of Martha's Vineyard.

Life began to change in the 1500s when European explorers, traders, and trappers arrived. Over the next few centuries, more people from Europe would arrive and transform the Wampanoag and other Native groups forever.

The Pilgrims Arrive

At the first contact with Europeans, it is estimated that there may have been as many as twelve thousand Wampanoag people. By the early seventeenth century, between 6,500 and 12,000 Wampanoag lived in this region. Their location in New England adversely affected them, however.

During this time, the Wampanoag included the Nauset of Cape Cod and the Sakonnet of southeastern Rhode Island. Various tribes of the islands, including Martha's Vineyard, the Elizabeth Islands, and Nantucket, were also counted among the Wampanoag. Their grand sachem, or principal leader, was Massasoit. At that time, the Wampanoag were known as the **Pokanoket**, after the name of Massasoit's home village, which was located at or near the present-day town of Warren, Rhode Island.

The first documented encounters between Europeans and Wampanoag occurred with the **Mashpee** Wampanoag of Cape Cod in the first decade of the seventeenth century. Martin Pring, Bartholomew Gosnold, and Samuel de Champlain met the Wampanoag as

The People and Culture of the Wampanoag

The Pilgrims arrived on the *Mayflower* in 1620.

they explored the coastline of Cape Cod. By 1620, the English had arrived in Virginia and set up a colony. Quickly, diseases carried by the early European seafarers devastated the Native populations in New England. The Wampanoag were so weakened by these diseases that they were more vulnerable to raids from the more northerly tribes, especially the Eastern Abenaki of Maine. Moreover, they were being pressed by the **Narragansett** of western Rhode Island, who had expanded eastward into Wampanoag territory after the disastrous epidemics from 1616 to 1619. Wampanoag towns such as Patuxet (Plymouth) were annihilated by illness and conflict.

Harried by other tribes, the Wampanoag allied themselves with the struggling but well-armed **Pilgrims**, who had arrived in Wampanoag territory in 1620. The Pilgrims were almost decimated after enduring a harsh winter; however, with the help of the Wampanoag, they survived. Fifty years of peace followed. More than a century later, President Abraham Lincoln proclaimed a national Thanksgiving holiday in 1863. However, for the Wampanoag, it was hardly a season to express gratitude. They mourned a great tragedy—the loss of their lands and loved ones—and the desperate struggle by those people who survived.

Giving Thanks

In the autumn of 1621, the Pilgrims invited Grand Sachem Massasoit and the Wampanoag people to join them in a feast now remembered as "the first Thanksgiving." However, only centuries later, in the nineteenth century, did this gathering come to be associated with the US holiday. The Thanksgiving of today more likely dates to a traditional English harvest festival that the Pilgrims celebrated in their new homeland. The feast evolved into a yearly autumn celebration in New England. In 1777, the Continental Congress recommended that the colonies set aside a day of Thanksgiving. In 1863, President Lincoln called for two days of Thanksgiving—one to be observed on August 6 to express gratitude for the Union victory at Gettysburg, and the other on the last Thursday in November to give thanks for the nation's bounty. Only the latter remains a US holiday.

Through the nineteenth century, the traditions of the holiday emphasized turkeys and family reunions, not Pilgrims and Native Americans. It was not until after the turn of the twentieth century that the pleasant image of colonists and Natives sharing a feast came to be admired. By World War I (1914–1918), popular art in schoolbooks, literature, and postcards firmly established the images of Pilgrims and New England Natives celebrating the first Thanksgiving—Pilgrims clothed in black and feathered Natives feasting on turkey, cranberries, and squash.

No Wampanoag accounts of the feast have been found. The only English written records come from William Bradford, governor of Plymouth Colony, and Edward Winslow, who took part in the first Thanksgiving. Bradford apparently proclaimed the celebration but does not mention the holiday in his book, *History of Plimoth Plantation*. Winslow does mention the thanksgiving feast in a letter to a friend in England dated December 11, 1621:

This painting shows
the first Thanksgiving
between settlers and
Native Americans.

The People and Culture of the Wampanoag

Our harvest being gotten in, our governor sent four men on fowling, that so we might after a more special manner rejoice together, after we had gathered the fruit of our labors. ... [For nearly a week] amongst other recreations, we exercised our arms, many of the Indians coming amongst us, and amongst the rest their greatest king Massasoit, with some ninety men, whom for three days we entertained and feasted, and they went out and killed five deer, which they brought to the plantation and bestowed on our governor, and upon the captain, and others.

Whatever its history, Thanksgiving—for most Americans—emphasizes the significant ideas of sharing and harmony. Yet, in view of the long record of broken promises, many Native leaders would agree with Russell Peters, former president of the Mashpee Wampanoag Indian Tribal Council, who said, "For Indians, Thanksgiving is now a day of fasting and mourning."

Following the days of the Pilgrims, the Wampanoag suffered greatly. Their story, however, is one of ultimate success, for they still exist today. Their cultural identity has been preserved and efforts are being made to bring back some forgotten traditions, as well as the original Wampanoag language. Today, many descendants of the Wampanoag continue to make their home in the region of their ancestors.

Ter-We-Lee-Ma, a Wampanoag member, wears a traditional headdress.

CHAPTER TWO

I am determined not to live until I have no country.

—Metacom, or "King Philip," Wampanoag chief

BUILDING A CIVILIZATION

Before the arrival of Europeans, the Wampanoag developed an intricate society. They had close family ties, dedicated warriors, and sturdy houses in which to live. Their lifestyles changed over time, but their identity as a people remained.

Village Life

The Wampanoag lived in villages. The people in each village made use of a particular region. During the winter, people lived in the main village, usually located in deep woods along

The Wampanoag lived in villages close to the coast. Here, a drawing from 1620 shows Wampanoag villages.

a stream or lake. When spring came, families took down their houses and moved separately or in small groups to outlying areas where food could be hunted, gathered, or cultivated.

During the spring fish runs, when thousands of spawning fish were swimming upstream, people left the main village and moved to camps near the rivers. People from several villages often camped on the banks, where they visited, played games, and enjoyed celebrations. In the summer, families dispersed into camps of one or more houses strung along the coast.

The People and Culture of the Wampanoag

They tended patches of corn and other crops near their summer camps and took short trips to pick fruits and berries and to catch lobsters. After the harvest in the early fall, people moved again, back to the main village. Even during the late autumn, families were often away at hunting camps. However, as the snows deepened, these families returned to the village to settle around their fires during the long, cold winter.

After the English established colonies in their territory, the Wampanoag often sought refuge in hilltop villages surrounded by a high wall known as a palisade. A palisade was made of sharpened poles stuck vertically into the ground and lashed together.

In the early seventeenth century, there were at least thirty Wampanoag villages. The villages were composed of circular lodges known as wigwams and rectangular dwellings known as longhouses. The family's cornfields were usually situated near their dwelling. Every village had a central open space for meetings and ceremonies, as well as a sweat lodge.

Housing

Dwellings known as **weetos** varied in size and shape. These smaller, dome-shaped wigwams were round at the base and about 15 feet (4.6 meters) in diameter. Larger, oblong or oval longhouses were about 30 feet (9 m) wide and 50 to 100 feet (15 to 30.5 m) long. These houses were large enough to shelter from forty to fifty people. Several families shared the larger dwellings when they came together in a winter village. When they were ocean fishing or gardening during

The Wampanoag built houses using the land around them.

The People and Culture of the Wampanoag

the other seasons, they took shelter in smaller weetos occupied by one or two families.

Both wigwams and longhouses were made of pole frames covered with woven mats or wide sheets of bark. Bark-covered lodges were warmer than mat-sheathed lodges. Winter dwellings were usually covered with bark, while the more portable houses in the seasonal camps were covered with mats. Wigwams were often set up over a shallow pit lined with cattails, pine needles, or other insulating materials. There were no windows. The only light came from a low doorway, often covered with a mat or sheet of bark, and a smoke hole in the roof, which could also be covered in rainy weather. A fire was built in a shallow hole in the center of the earthen floor. A longhouse had an entrance at each end and a row of smoke holes along the roof. Each family had its own fire, and there was a row of fire pits for cooking meals and providing warmth in the winter.

Bulrush mats, often decorated with paintings, lined the interior walls. Mats were also used as bedding on the floor of the wigwam. In a longhouse, mats for bedding were arranged on raised platforms along the walls. About 1.5 feet (0.2 m) above the floor, these platforms were made of forked posts stuck in the ground to support horizontal poles. Furs served as blankets. A large bed accommodated an entire family and any visitors. Inside the dwelling, there were bundles of rushes, hemp, and other materials for making mats and baskets, along with tools and weapons.

Other furnishings included baskets, bags, clay pots, birch-bark boxes, and containers for food storage and preparation. People ate meals with carved wooden bowls, plates, and spoons. Pots were hung over the fire from a square frame made of forked branches supporting slender poles. Cooking pots were originally clay, but the Wampanoag later traded with Europeans for durable iron, brass, or copper kettles. There was always a pot of simmering food or a hunk of meat slowly roasting over the fire so that people could eat whenever they were hungry. During damp weather, fish and meat were dried on wooden racks placed near the fire.

Chiefs had larger, more elaborately furnished homes than did the other villagers. Poor people had to take shelter in small huts. The Wampanoag also built large dance houses that could be 100 or 200 feet (30.5 to 61 m) long. Other village structures included watch houses in the cornfields, where people shooed away hungry birds, and menstrual huts, where women retired for a few days every month.

Sweat lodges were also part of the village. Individuals purified themselves in these buildings. The Wampanoag made sweat lodges by excavating a small cave in a hillside, over which a wooden structure was erected and covered with mats. This formed an interior about 8 feet (2.4 m) in diameter and 4 feet (1.2 m) high. Rocks were heated over a fire until the sweat lodge became very hot. The sweat lodge was located near a stream or lake so that people could run out and plunge into the cold water.

Nearly fifty years after the landing of the Pilgrims, most Wampanoag were still living in weetos. But they gradually adopted European-style frame houses with shingled roofs.

The Wampanoag wore and traded wampum.

Community

Wampanoag society had three basic social classes:
the sachem and the members of his family; the other
members of the community; and the war captives who
lived as servants. Within the first and second of these
categories, there were great differences in wealth and
social position. The wealthy and noble people had the
finest mats in their houses. They had striking tattoos on
their faces and wore considerable **wampum** on their
bodies. Men of these classes often had more than one
wife and servants.

A sachem governed a certain territory. Sub-sachems
were responsible for smaller areas and villages within
that territory. A sachem inherited his position through the
male line—that is, a son succeeded his father upon his

This woodcut shows a Wampanoag warrior in traditional clothing.

Building a Civilization

death. Occasionally, the wife of a sachem assumed the position when he died. Daughters and nephews could also become sachems if the leader's son was too young. The position was then held for the son until he came of age. The sachem oversaw the allotment of land and collected tribute from his followers. A sachem with more followers enjoyed greater wealth, so a leader tried to please his people. Otherwise, they might leave and join another sachem. A sub-sachem attended to the personal needs of his group, such as resolving disputes.

Although a sachem was supposed to have absolute power, on important matters a tribal council of village and **clan** chiefs, known as **pnieses**, advised him. The village and clan chiefs also served as war leaders and personal guards for the sachem when he traveled. The sachem also consulted respected elders and shamans, called **powwows**.

Villages were independent of each other but sometimes formed alliances. After mysterious, deadly epidemics decimated Native populations between 1616 and 1619, the Wampanoag became more unified as a people. The Wampanoag call this era the "Great Dying," when thousands of Native people perished.

Wampanoag society was also organized by family and clan. Like many other Native people of eastern North America, families were matrilineal, meaning that people traced their ancestry through the mother's side. The Wampanoag were further organized into a number of clans whose members traced their descent from a common ancestor.

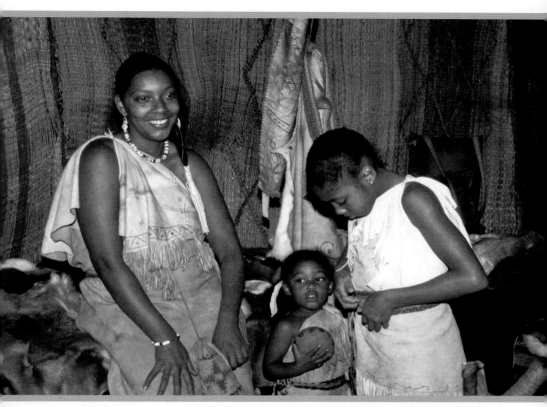

Wampanoag adults pass the traditions and history of their people to younger generations.

The Wampanoag lived this way for centuries before their first encounter with Europeans. Some of their traditional housing structures and practices remain part of modern-day Wampanoag life, but many aspects were forgotten over time with the influence of European customs, language, and beliefs.

Chief Metacom, also called King Philip, was a respected Wampanoag leader.

CHAPTER THREE

Wampum ... sustains our health, critiques our history, and adorns our apparel.

—Joan Avant Tavares, Mashpee Wampanoag

LIFE IN A WAMPANOAG VILLAGE

Along with a specific way of operating their society, the Wampanoag had special traditions and practices. They followed a seasonal cycle of hunting, fishing, gathering, planting, and harvesting. They noted the passage of time by observing the celestial bodies and the four seasons. The time of day was measured by the height of the sun, the months were determined by the phases of the moon, and the seasons were marked by the changing weather. Similarly, they had organized rituals dedicated to birth, puberty, and death.

Life Cycle

The life cycle, from birth to death, was sacred to the Wampanoag. Their ceremonies and traditions were central to the Wampanoag way of life.

Being Born

A woman continued to work in the fields and village until she was about to give birth. She then retired to a lodge where, with the help of one or more older women serving as midwives, she had her baby. If she had problems in the delivery, a powwow was asked to call upon powerful spirits for assistance.

Wampanoag women carried their babies in cradleboards such as this.

The newborn was coated with grease and clothed in a beaver skin or other soft fur, then wrapped onto a **cradleboard**. For most of the day, the baby remained safely on the cradleboard, always close to its mother. The mother carried the baby on her back as she worked outside. When inside, she leaned the cradleboard against the wall of the lodge, where the infant could watch her as she cooked meals.

The Wampanoag ate a variety of fruit from the area around them.

The mother often sang soothing lullabies to her baby. Usually quiet and content, babies seldom cried. The mother nursed her baby for at least a year, after which she began to give the child small morsels of food.

Growing Up

The Wampanoag were very fond of their children. Children were rarely disciplined but instead were taught through a positive example. One English colonist thought that the children were "sawcie, bold, and undutifull." However, the Wampanoag wished their children to be not only respectful but also spirited and independent.

Children learned by watching and imitating their parents and other adults as they worked at various chores. Boys shot small bows and arrows to practice skills they would need in hunting and warfare. Girls played with small cooking pots and helped plant and tend crops from an early age.

Children enjoyed playing many kinds of games. They also learned about the beliefs and traditions of the Wampanoag by listening to stories told by their parents and grandparents.

Maturing

As children approached adulthood, they underwent initiation ceremonies. There were ceremonies for girls, but little is known about them today. More is known about rituals for boys entering adulthood.

When a boy experienced puberty, he was blindfolded and taken into the wilderness during the fall. He was left there with a bow and arrows, a hatchet, and a knife. He had to provide for himself through the winter, when game was scarce. Toward spring, the men of the village went to find the young man and take him home. Afterward, he was sent out every morning with a knowledgeable man to gather herbs and roots. He learned to make a bitter and poisonous tea from the plant juices, along with an antidote. Once he was able to withstand a dose of this tea, the men and women sang and danced. The young man was then considered an adult.

At the time of initiation, both girls and boys received their new adult names. They were then ready for marriage.

Marrying

When a man wanted to marry, he first spoke with the woman and then with her parents. The village leader also had to approve of the marriage. The man gave the bride's parents wampum or other goods as payment for the loss of their daughter. The man's parents and other relatives might help him by contributing some of these gifts.

Prominent families built alliances through political marriages between sachems and women of high standing from other villages. Sachems often had two or more wives. Anyone wealthy enough to support several wives was highly esteemed. Most men had one wife.

If a woman's husband mistreated her, she could leave him. A husband could banish an unfaithful wife. However, people seldom lived alone. Widows, widowers, and divorced individuals usually moved in with their relatives until they married again.

Dying

The dead were placed in a sitting position in a grave lined with mats. Weapons, tools, wampum, ornaments, and other belongings needed in the afterlife were buried with the body. The grave was located in or near the house of the deceased. The sheathing was removed from the weeto, leaving only the frame, and was then abandoned.

Painting their faces black, men and women mourned the loss of their loved ones. Gathering around the grave, family and friends cried in grief and mourned for many days. When a sachem or other prominent individual died, people mourned for a year.

It was believed that the souls of good people upon their death journeyed to the southwest, a spirit world, where they would live as they had in the physical world. During this journey to the spirit world, the deceased faced many hazards, including a vicious dog. The souls of the less fortunate were condemned to wander, lost and restless, in the world. People believed that these restless, unhappy ghosts lingered near camps and villages, inflicting misfortune and illness on the living. However, once they reached the afterlife, the souls of good, contented people enjoyed an idyllic life.

Warring

The Wampanoag traditionally allied with the Massachusett [sic] tribe. Wampanoag enemies included the Eastern Abenaki and the Narragansett, and later the English colonists. Before going to war, men painted their faces—either all black, black and white, black and red, or spotted with a variety of colors—to make themselves appear fearsome to their enemies. They fought with wooden bows and arrows tipped with stone, bone, eagle claw, or crab-tail points. Wielding ball-headed war clubs, they protected themselves with bark shields. Leaders often carried long spears. Warriors used sharp knives to take scalps.

It is believed that the pnieses formed a prestigious military society. Members of this society provided leadership in battle. Boys who showed promise of great strength and good character—especially courage, honesty, and judgment—were selected to become pnieses. These young men endured rigorous training. When deemed ready, they were initiated into the society in a ceremony in which they underwent daunting physical and spiritual ordeals. Bold and courageous, pnieses considered themselves impervious to the weapons of their enemies.

The Wampanoag went to war for many reasons, including to avenge a murder and to settle disputes over territory and power struggles among leaders. The sachem or a group within the community could call

Wampanoag weapons included axes and clubs.

for a war. The sachem and his council then met and decided whether to undertake the war. Once it was decided to go to war, the warriors danced and listened to speeches and readied themselves for battle. As the warriors approached the enemy camp, they slipped from one tree to another. Whenever possible, they tried to make a surprise attack when their opponents were sleeping or taking shelter during a storm. After the attack, the warriors just as quickly retreated with their plunder and prisoners. Captives were often tortured and killed. Some, especially women and children, were adopted into the tribe. When they returned to their village, the warriors celebrated their victory.

The Wampanoag people hunted animals such as foxes for their furs.

The People and Culture of the Wampanoag

Fishing and Hunting

The coastal region of southern New England abounded in wildlife, both in the water and on the land. In the spring, people gathered at the falls of rivers to catch herring and other fish migrating upstream in spawning runs. They used spears, nets, and lines fitted with bone hooks. Sometimes, they built weirs across the streams. They also caught freshwater fish, such as trout, perch, pike, catfish, and occasionally, large sturgeon. People remained in the fishing camps until planting time, when they moved to the coast to tend small fields. There, through the summer and into the fall, they caught saltwater fish, including bass, cod, and haddock. After moving inland for the winter, they occasionally caught fish through holes in the ice on ponds and lakes. However, in Rhode Island, the Wampanoag continued to fish in the ocean through the cold months. Fish were eaten fresh or dried and then stored for use in the lean months of winter.

During the spring migration, men hunted ducks, Canada geese, and swans. Hunters netted turkeys, ruffed grouse, pigeons, and cranes, or shot them with bows and arrows. At night, they snatched cormorants from their roosts on the offshore rocks. They also caught turtles for their delicious meat. People sometimes butchered whales stranded on the beach. In warm weather, they caught seals, valued for their meat and oil, while the animals slept on the rocks. Women trapped lobsters, whose meat was used for fish bait or dried and smoked for winter use. They also gathered shellfish, such as oysters, clams, and scallops, which they cooked over heated rocks or dried and stored for the winter.

Men hunted game, ranging in size from gray squirrels to black bears. Otters, muskrats, beavers, raccoons, foxes, wolves, and an occasional moose were also hunted or trapped. However, they mostly hunted white-tailed deer, the animal that supplied most of the meat in their diet. Men stalked deer and caught them in traps and snares throughout the year, but they especially hunted these fleet-footed animals in the fall and early winter. Men, women, and children sometimes joined in large, communal hunts in which they drove a large number of deer into a V-shaped fence, 1 or 2 miles (1.6 to 3.2 kilometers) long and made of brush and branches. The deer were chased through the wide opening and toward the narrow end, where hunters had set traps or shot the confined animals.

When the snow began to sweep over the land, people moved back to their main villages in the woods and valleys where they were shielded from the cold winds. From December or January until April, they

RECIPE
CRANBERRY CRISP

Cranberries taste delicious in many dishes, including desserts. Here is a tasty recipe that is a favorite at the Fall Social on Cranberry Day.

INGREDIENTS

4 cups (800 grams) whole fresh cranberries
2 cups (340 g) brown sugar
2 cups (340 g) flour
1 cup (140 g) uncooked oatmeal
1 stick butter (113 g), cut into pieces
pinch of cinnamon

Mix together the cranberries, 1 cup (220 g) brown sugar, 1 cup (128 g) flour, and cinnamon. Place this mixture in a well-greased baking pan or dish. Mix 1 cup (220 g) brown sugar, 1 cup (128 g) flour, the oatmeal, and stick of butter. Spread this mixture over the cranberries and bake at 375°F (190°C) until the top is brown and the fruit bubbles—about 35 minutes.

settled in these winter villages. They occasionally trapped game but lived mostly on their stores of food.

Tending the Land

In early spring, the Wampanoag tapped maple trees for sap that they cooked down to make sweet syrup. Through the spring, summer, and fall, women gathered roots, berries, fruits, and nuts. Roots were stored as winter food, while wild strawberries, blackberries, raspberries, blueberries, and grapes were eaten fresh. Currants and other berries were dried and stored for later use. In the autumn, women collected acorns, walnuts, and chestnuts, all of which were shelled, dried, and stored for use when food was scarce. These nuts were pounded into flour and added to soups and stews. Acorns had to be thoroughly boiled to remove the bitter taste. Cranberries were picked in the low-lying ground on Martha's Vineyard and in southern New England. Hemp was gathered to make nets, fishing lines, ropes, and twined baskets.

The Wampanoag raised corn, beans, pumpkins, and squash. Corn became their most important crop. The kernels had a variety of colors, including red, blue, yellow, and white.

The first European visitors were impressed by the number of well-tended fields along the shores and villages. To clear land for a new field, men chopped down trees with stone axes, leaving stumps about 3 feet (0.9 m) above the ground. They burned the trunks and branches, and then the women planted seeds among the stumps. Over time, as the stumps rotted, they were rooted out and lugged from the fields. In preparation for planting, women loosened the soil with clamshell hoes. Then they made small hills about 3 feet (0.9 m) apart using horseshoe crab shells. In each hill, they placed three or four kernels of corn and the same number of beans. They often buried small fish in the hills as fertilizer. Throughout the growing season, they diligently cultivated the fields with hoes. After several years, a field was sometimes allowed to lie fallow, or unplanted, to recover its fertility. Then the brush was burned away and the field was planted again. Women usually did all of the planting, cultivating, and harvesting, although children and old men sometimes helped. The only crop grown by the men was tobacco, for use in rituals.

As the corn ripened, watch houses were built in the fields where women or older children chased away the hungry birds. Sometimes, hawks were caught, tamed, and kept near the fields to scare the other birds away. Some corn was picked and eaten fresh, like sweet corn, but most of the crop was allowed to fully ripen and the kernels to become hard. In the autumn, this hard corn and the other crops were harvested. Some of the harvest was eaten fresh, but most of it was dried for later use. Women placed the dried corn, beans, and squash in woven sacks or baskets and stored them in caches, or underground pits, lined with mats. The pits were covered with mats and sometimes planks. These provisions were used as needed during the fall and winter. The first Pilgrims on Cape Cod sometimes found these caches and raided them.

Meat and fish were usually boiled or roasted on a forked stick. Small pieces of dried or fresh meat, fish, and shellfish were added to soups and stews. Clam juice was used as a seasoning in place of salt. Ears of fresh corn were boiled, while kernels of hard corn were parched, or dried, over hot coals and ground into a coarse meal. This cornmeal was added to stews or cooked into a thick porridge. Cornmeal was also made into a dough flavored with crushed strawberries, then shaped into loaves, wrapped in leaves, and baked in ashes to make bread. Cornmeal and powdered dried currants were boiled and made into cakes, which the Wampanoag favored.

Clothes

Women made all the clothing for their families from animal skins. Deer, which were abundant in the woods and fields, provided the most popular materials. Deerskins were tough yet thin enough to be made pliable by tanning into **buckskin**. Deerskins were also large enough so that clothing could be made without sewing many pieces together. Moose skins were sometimes used to make clothing, but these heavy hides were better suited for moccasins.

Deer hides were first scraped to remove the hair and flesh. Then the rawhide was tanned into buckskin by laboriously working oils into the material until it became soft. The buckskin was then smoked over a fire to give it a tan color. If buckskin leggings, shirts, and dresses got wet, they could be wrung out and hung by the fire to dry without becoming stiff. If a deer was killed in winter, the thick coat of hair was usually left on. These hides were used for cloaks and bedding.

Wampanoag men and women wear traditional deerskin clothing.

Life in a Wampanoag Village

Women wore wraparound skirts tied with a belt, and blouses that hung from the shoulders. They also wore moccasins. After European contact, they wore dresses made of two deerskins sewn together and with straps at the shoulders. Men wore buckskin **breechcloths** and moccasins. Buckskin clothing was often decorated with quillwork. During the summer, everyone went barefoot but carried moccasins in case they had to travel over rough ground. Both men and women wore buckskin leggings when traveling through scratchy undergrowth. Leggings were also worn during cold weather, especially by the elderly.

Men and women often wore animal skin capes, drawn under the right arm and over the left shoulder. When traveling, the robe was tightly cinched with a belt. The bare shoulder was covered by another piece in cold weather. Women's capes were nearly twice as long as those for men. During the summer, they wore deerskin capes sewn with the fur side out. Winter robes were made of deer, beaver, otter, raccoon, bear, and fox skins sewn together with the fur inside. They also made cloaks of woven turkey feathers, hemp, or grass.

Men and women liked to wear jewelry. They adorned themselves with shell and bone necklaces and brass or copper earrings. Men wore breastplates and **bandoliers** made of flat, hammered brass or copper. Breastplates were sometimes made of rows of copper tubes about 4 inches (10 centimeters) long and 0.25 inches (0.64 cm) in diameter. Shorter copper tubes were strung together for headbands and necklaces.

The People and Culture of the Wampanoag

Hairstyles and Decorations

The Wampanoag smeared their skin with animal grease or vegetable oil as protection against insects and the cold. Both men and women carefully combed and oiled their hair every day. Generally, they wore their hair long, and it was believed that wearing a ponytail made it grow faster. Women often cut their hair when they got married and wore a head covering until the hair grew back. Young men who were not yet warriors usually had short hair. People sometimes cut bangs in the front and wore the rest of their hair either loose or braided. Some men may have pulled out all of their hair except for a scalp lock. They decorated their hair with turkey or eagle feathers, foxtails, strips of hide dyed red, and other ornaments.

By the early 1600s, wampum had become the most popular type of shell beads used in ornaments. Wampum was most often fashioned from the quahog, or hard-shelled clam. Tubular beads were cut from whole shells. A hole was then made in each bead with a stone drill. After Europeans introduced metal tools, the holes were made with metal drills. Belts of these small purple and white shell beads were also used as a kind of money. People wore bracelets, necklaces, headbands, and belts made of wampum. Collars, caps, and ear pendants were also made of wampum.

The Wampanoag also adorned themselves with tattoos and body paint. To create a tattoo, a sharp instrument was used to lift and pierce the skin and a black pigment was rubbed into the wound. Figures of animals, such as bears, deer, moose, wolves, eagles, or hawks, were applied, most often on the cheeks. People also branded geometric shapes on the arms and chest with a hot iron.

Before painting their bodies, the Wampanoag greased themselves to provide a bond for the dry pigment. Then they applied a dry pigment of red, yellow, white, or black powder to their skins. Red pigment was most often used in the hair. The face was painted with multiple colors or a single color. During times of mourning, people painted their faces black with soot and ashes. Warriors painted themselves when they were about to go into battle. Both men and women painted their faces for ceremonies and games.

Arts and Crafts

The Wampanoag crafted many of the tools, weapons, and household objects needed in their daily life from wood. Men shaped wood into bows and arrow shafts, while women made hoes with wooden handles and clamshell blades. The inner bark, or bast, from trees was woven into baskets and other goods. From pine bark, they obtained red dye, turpentine, and pitch. Some artisans were especially skilled at carving wooden bowls and spoons from burls, which had the advantage of not being easily split along the grain.

People used birch bark to make a variety of objects, including boxes and canoes. To make a swift, graceful canoe, sheets of birch bark were sewn over a wood frame and the seams were sealed with pine pitch. Most often, however, men labored long hours to make dugout canoes. Some were as long as 50 feet (15 m) and large enough to hold forty people, although most carried about ten to fifteen people. The men first chopped down a tree with a stone ax. Then, over the course of ten to twelve days, they hollowed out the trunk with small, controlled fires. They smoothed the inside with shell scrapers and shaped the outside with stone hatchets. Finally, they sanded the entire craft with a rough stone.

Women used buckskin not only for making clothes, but also for fashioning pouches for carrying tobacco and personal objects and for storing food. They also made a variety of everyday objects from various plant materials, such as bulrushes, bent grass, cornhusks, hemp, and flag leaves. Women wove bulrushes or flag leaves into mats and sewed the mats together with hemp thread and a bone needle. Mats served as sheathing for houses and as lining for the floor. Fine mats were used for sitting. Food was spread out on fine mats to dry.

The Wampanoag were skilled in making soft and smooth, yet strong cords. Cord was usually made from hemp. Long fibers from the stem were braided until they had attained the desired length and thickness of thread, string, or rope. The thread was used in weaving baskets, sewing together mats, and making capes of twisted turkey feathers. People used cords of twisted fibers to lash together the framework of their weetos. Hemp strings were used as fishing lines or looped into fishnets. Cords were woven into large bags for storing food.

The Wampanoag developed several methods of basket weaving throughout history.

Baskets and Other Objects

Women wove baskets in many sizes and shapes from grasses and rushes. They also used strips of wood. Weavers used two basic techniques—twining and plaiting. In twining, horizontal pieces of hemp cord, known as the weft, were wrapped around the more rigid pieces of bulrushes, called the warp. In the plaited technique, also known as splint basketry, both the weft and the warp were rigid strips of wood such as strips of ash or white oak. The splints were woven alternately over and under to create a checkerboard pattern. Over time, splint baskets became more common and eventually were the only kind of basket made by the

Wampanoag. These baskets were made for use during the corn harvest. One splint basket was carried on the back and another larger basket was placed at the edge of the field. Splint baskets were also used as sieves for sifting cornmeal. Small baskets were used for carrying parched cornmeal on journeys, and corn was placed in large baskets in storage pits.

The Wampanoag made dishes and other objects from clay, stone, and minerals. They collected quartz and slate for making tools and weapons. From various outcroppings, they quarried other minerals, such as limonite and hematite, from which they extracted yellow and red pigments. From soft soapstone they carved bowls and pipes. The Wampanoag traded pottery, wooden bowls, and wampum with other Native peoples in exchange for copper to be fashioned into ornaments. From Europeans they obtained metal pots and kettles and learned to cast pewter, brass, and lead into ornaments, buttons, and ammunition.

Clay for making pots was readily available around Plymouth and at Aquinnah, which was later called Gay Head because of the colorful clay found at the cliffs. The Wampanoag shaped these brilliant clays into pots, bowls, and jugs. The objects were then sun-dried instead of fired, because firing in a kiln dulled the colors. Pottery is still one of the most distinctive and striking of Wampanoag handicrafts.

Today, the Wampanoag continue the traditions of their ancestors. Many customs and ceremonies are still celebrated, and people still make baskets. Some of the baskets from older generations are on display in museums in the United States and around the world.

This drawing shows a Wampanoag shaman practicing medicine inside a wigwam.

CHAPTER FOUR

Each one of us is a special gift to each other because we've got something to share.

—John Peters, Wampanoag chief

BELIEFS OF THE WAMPANOAG

The Wampanoag had many beliefs and practices that guided them in daily life and through hard times. From spiritual beliefs to social gatherings, these practices brought people together and helped create a community. Some of these activities continue to be celebrated today.

Spirituality

The Wampanoag recognized a supreme being and creator known as **Kiehtan** and many lesser gods. The Wampanoag believed that all of creation—the plants, the animals, and the earth itself—was imbued with spirits. Striving to live in harmony with the woods and the water around them, they did not distinguish between the physical and spiritual aspects of the natural world. People did not believe themselves to be superior to animals. They respected all other living creatures. When deer were hunted and plants harvested, the Wampanoag acknowledged their sacrifice and expressed gratitude to the spirit of the animal or plant.

People believed that various spirits could use supernatural powers known as *manitous* to help or hinder them. Animals, plants, or even objects such as rocks could have manitous. An individual would have good fortune if he glimpsed, touched, or dreamed about a manitou that was symbolized by one of these spirits. The Wampanoag strongly believed in the significance of dreams. A bad dream was regarded as a warning or threat from the supernatural, and when the dreamer awakened, he immediately prayed for help. If the dream was particularly ominous, he asked his friends to watch over him. He offered food to them but fasted himself and remained awake for several days and nights. In a good dream, one's fortune would be improved, especially if a guardian spirit appeared. This guardian spirit could be called upon whenever help was needed.

Rituals and Celebrations

Blending religion and medicine, powwows were responsible for healing the spirit and the body. The term *powwow* refers to a shamanic method of acquiring power. A man—and occasionally a woman—became a powwow through a dream in which an animal spirit chose him or her. (The **Algonquian** term *powwow* has come to mean a modern Native American festival.) The individual then announced the dream to others in the community and a two-day celebration was held. With the help of their own animal spirits, powwows conducted rituals and treated illnesses and injuries with herbal medicines. They also mediated with the spirit world to help with these cures and to forecast the weather.

Throughout the year, the Wampanoag held ceremonies that included feasting, singing, dancing, and playing games. On many occasions, they gave thanks for an abundant harvest, good health, and peace. At least twice a year, several Wampanoag bands came together for a large gathering. Every spring, they held a celebration at the fish camps. In the fall, they enjoyed a harvest festival in which everyone danced through the night. There were also small private feasts, notably the Nikomo or Nickommo, held in the winter. A family invited a small group of guests to this feast, at which the host gave away much of his wealth. During times of hardships—war, drought, famine, and illness—the Wampanoag gathered to call upon the spirits for assistance. They offered prayers until the drought was broken or the other adversity was ended. In all these

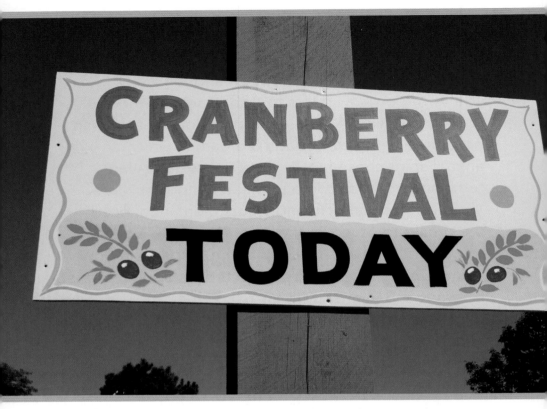

Every year, the Cranberry Festival brings large groups of visitors to the Wampanoag reservations.

ceremonies, people danced, sang, and offered gifts to please the spirits.

Today, the Wampanoag hold ceremonies to honor the traditions of their ancestors. Every year, these festivals bring together the Native community, and local and international communities. In the autumn, everyone gathers for Cranberry Day, the most important annual event for the Wampanoag living on Martha's Vineyard. Parents and children harvest cranberries during the morning, and in the afternoon, they gather around a fire to listen to stories. In the evening, people eat a dinner, followed by singing, dancing, and giving thanks.

The People and Culture of the Wampanoag

Fun and Games

The Wampanoag enjoyed playing games and gambling. Their most important team sport was called "football" by the English. Posts set about 1 mile (1.6 km) apart on the long sandy beaches served as goals. Players tried to get a ball about the size of a tennis ball over the opponent's goal without using their hands. Men put their weapons aside but still painted themselves as though going to war. The competition was fierce. In the rough play, bones were often broken. The contest might go on for two days before a team scored a goal and the game was over. Betting on the outcome was heavy. When tribes played against each other, the goalposts were hung with a wealth of wagered goods, including wampum. Large crowds of women, children, and old men gathered to watch the game and cheer for their team. Despite the vigorous play, there were few quarrels and after the game, everyone gathered for a great feast.

Individuals also challenged each other to contests of strength and skill in archery, running, and swimming. Such contests usually attracted large audiences, especially when members of different tribes competed. Many bets were placed. People were especially interested in marksmanship contests with bows and arrows. English visitors were impressed with the skill and endurance of the swimmers. Similarly, Wampanoag runners balanced speed with endurance, running great distances for a full day or more.

The Wampanoag played a gambling game called hubhub. In hubhub, five bone dice, painted black on

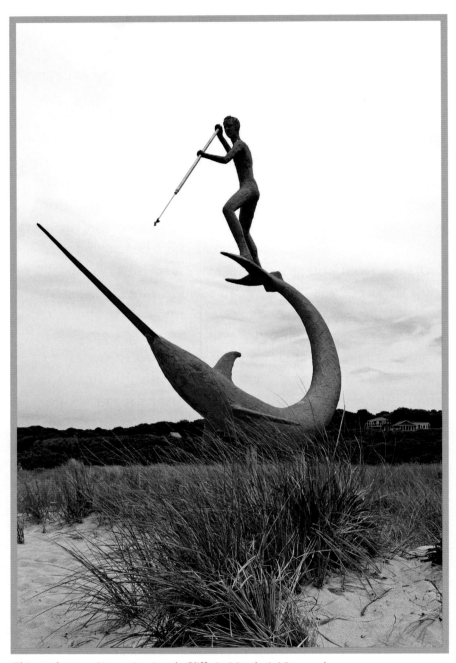

This sculpture sits on Aquinnah Cliffs in Martha's Vineyard.

The People and Culture of the Wampanoag

one side and white on the other, were placed in a wooden dish. The dish was struck hard on the ground to make the dice bounce in the air. People bet on what combination of colors would turn up. When hubhub was played between teams from different villages, an arbor of four long poles was built for each team. These poles were draped with wampum that was wagered on the game. Hundreds of people came to watch hubhub contests held between villages.

Men, in particular, loved games and gambling. They avidly competed against each other even when there was no audience. A group of men could become engrossed in a game all day and through the night without pausing to sleep or eat. They called upon the spirits to help them win and sometimes carried a rock crystal charm, thought to be a piece of a thunderbolt, to improve their chances. Men might gamble away all their belongings, even the moccasins on their feet. Despite the intense competition, they usually parted company peacefully.

The Importance of Stories

Stories helped people to understand their history and heritage. Among the favorite stories were those about the supernatural deeds of Moshup. Whenever a fog settles over the coastal waters, the Wampanoag believe that it is Moshup's way of reminding people that he is still there, watching over them.

According to the Wampanoag, Moshup not only formed the island of Martha's Vineyard, but he also showed people many ways in which they could provide for themselves. Here is a short story about Moshup and how he taught the people how to hunt whales, known as *pottap*:

> Moshup became the first whaler in Aquinnah when he caught whales as they swam near shore. He took the whales to his den and often invited others in the Wampanoag community to join him in a great feast. To cook the pottap, he yanked up trees and built a great fire. Today, trees are scarce on Aquinnah because Moshup used so many to stoke the fires of his feasts.
>
> Moshup taught the Wampanoag to follow schools of blackfish to locate the whales. Many of his children and followers took up whaling, too.

Today, the Wampanoag still pass down the tales and traditions of their ancestors. Every summer, the Legends of Moshup Pageant, held at Aquinnah, feature people dressed in traditional Wampanoag clothing and the telling of ancestral stories. This is a popular event, drawing many to Martha's Vineyard each year.

Today, Aquinnah remains one of the most scenic areas of Massachusetts, deeply connected to the Wampanoag people.

With the arrival
of Europeans, the
Wampanoag way of
life changed.

CHAPTER FIVE

We are still the first people of this land.

—We Still Live Here documentary

OVERCOMING HARDSHIPS

The men, women, and children of the Wampanoag followed certain beliefs and lived a certain lifestyle for hundreds of years. Then, in the 1600s, people from across the Atlantic Ocean arrived, and the Wampanoag's lifestyle was challenged.

The first Europeans introduced many new concepts to the Native world. One of these was a new religion, called Christianity. Men and women from Europe preached to the Wampanoag and converted many to their religion. Today, many Wampanoag remain Christians but have incorporated some ancient beliefs into their modern lifestyles and traditions.

Along with religion, the Europeans changed the Wampanoag's way of life. Many times, these changes were drastic, and led to conflicts between Natives and settlers, as the Natives tried to resist efforts to change their identities and struggled to preserve their culture.

The Pilgrims

Among the first Europeans to encounter the Wampanoag were the Pilgrims. This was a group of people who fled England for the New World, having suffered religious persecution for their own lifestyles and practices. Their ship, the *Mayflower*, landed at Plymouth Rock in September 1620.

The Pilgrims were quickly greeted by the encroaching fall and winter weather, and did not have much time to plant or harvest crops or build sturdy structures. The Wampanoag, however, had lived in the area for generations and had adapted to the climate. They also had worked the land to create successful crops.

When they learned strangers had arrived on the coast, the Wampanoag were curious but at first kept their distance, Eventually, Grand Sachem Massasoit, who ruled over all the Wampanoag, sent a man named Squanto as an envoy and translator to the Pilgrims. Squanto soon earned a reputation and kinship with the Pilgrims for his ability to speak English. Several years earlier, Squanto had been kidnapped and taken to Europe, where he learned the language. When he was taken back to North America, Squanto escaped

The Pilgrims met the Wampanoag and Algonquin tribes shortly after their first winter at Plymouth Rock.

and returned to the Wampanoag. It is believed that he surprised the Pilgrims by speaking English when he encountered them on the beach.

Massasoit helped the inexperienced newcomers during their first hard winter in the New World and generally tried to live peacefully with them. He agreed to a treaty of friendship with the Pilgrims, mostly out of necessity because many of his people had died in the Great Dying a few years earlier. He also hoped to forge an alliance with the Pilgrims against a neighboring tribe, the Narragansett. The Wampanoag helped the Pilgrims grow crops and to provide for themselves. In turn, the Pilgrims traded European goods, such as iron kettles and metal knives, to the Wampanoag.

A Peaceful People

As other colonies were founded in New England in the 1600s, the Wampanoag remained peaceful. They even befriended Roger Williams, a prominent theologian, who rebelled against many of the teachings of a religious sect called the **Puritans**. Accused of heresy, Williams fled Salem, Massachusetts, and the Massachusetts Bay Colony to establish the colony of Providence Plantations in what is now Rhode Island. During his journey, he got caught in a snowstorm and would most likely have perished if the Wampanoag had not found and sheltered him. Williams met Massasoit when the grand sachem was about thirty years old. Williams later declared that the two men quickly became "great friends." Williams also befriended Canonicus, the elderly leader of the Narragansett, and traveled the woods for days with both chiefs.

Metacom's War

By the mid-1600s, tensions were mounting between the New England colonists and the Native peoples. The colonists wanted more land for themselves, while the Native people thought the land should be shared with everyone. When Massasoit died in 1661, he was succeeded by his son Wamsutta, also called Alexander. Ordered to report to the English at Plymouth, Wamsutta died on his way home. Some said he had been poisoned. Massasoit's second son, Metacom, then became sachem of the Wampanoag. He came to be known as Philip and sometimes as King Philip. He renewed peace with the English, but relations became strained as colonists further encroached on Wampanoag lands and devastated the forests and game.

The English pushed the declining Native peoples into smaller communities or forced them into "praying towns," villages established by ministers. The colonists also deceived the Wampanoag, often with the use of alcohol—which was both appealing and addicting to many Native Americans—into giving up their lands. Sickness swept through the villages. The Wampanoag did not have immunity to diseases such as smallpox, and it was not long before that epidemic ravaged Native American villages. In 1671, there were about forty thousand colonists in New England, while the Native population, which included the Wampanoag, had dwindled to about twenty thousand people. The farm fields and pastures of the colonists spread, driving away game and angering the Wampanoag. By 1675, the Wampanoag had one remaining strip of land, which the colonists also wanted.

This engraving shows King Philip.

The People and Culture of the Wampanoag

"Soon after I became sachem they disarmed all my people," Philip declared. "I am determined not to live until I have no country." Having reached a breaking point, he led his people, who had moved to the area around present-day Bristol, Rhode Island, in an effort to unite all the tribes in southern New England in what came to be known as **King Philip's War**. The war broke out on June 20, 1675, at the settlement of Swansea and quickly spread across southern New England. The Wampanoag, allied with the Narragansett and other Native peoples, hoped to drive the British completely out of their territory. Considered a brilliant military strategist, Philip led Wampanoag and Narragansett warriors in many victories at the beginning of the war and nearly succeeded in destroying the colonies. Hundreds of colonists were slaughtered—nearly half the population of English settlers. However, some warriors began to fight before the campaign had been completely prepared, leading many warriors to refuse to join the alliance. Betrayed by traitors and cut off from supplies, Philip retreated to the cedar swamps of Rhode Island. In August 1676, he was defeated and killed in battle, effectively ending the offensive campaign in southern New England.

Aftermath of the War

Colonial militia then ruthlessly hunted down and killed Wampanoag and other Native peoples, including those who had remained neutral or friendly during the war. After a few months of fierce fighting, the English finally prevailed. The heads of Philip and Weetamo, Wamsutta's widow, were displayed on posts as a warning. Most of the Natives remaining in the area were either killed or enslaved. Many widows and children were sold as slaves in the West Indies. Philip's son was auctioned off with about five hundred other Native people. The Wampanoag and Narragansett, in particular, were nearly wiped out.

A handful of survivors managed to escape to the interior—some journeying as far as the Great Lakes region and Canada. Others fled to Cape Cod and nearby islands, where they joined Wampanoag communities that had not taken part in the war. Both friendly Natives and enemy warriors were forced onto reservations called plantations. For centuries after this conflict, the Wampanoag suffered mistreatment as servants and discrimination in general. At best, they were forgotten and ignored. In some instances, they were not able to survive in a rapidly changing world. The Native population on Nantucket Island declined from about 1,500 in 1600 to 358 in 1763, and then to only 20 people in 1792, mainly as a result of disease. The last Native person there died in 1855.

The Wampanoag in other areas of New England fared somewhat better. The people living at Mashpee, Cape Cod, were granted 50 square miles (130 square kilometers) of land as a plantation in 1660. They fought to establish and maintain their own self-governed community. Over the years, Wampanoag people from other areas of the Cape came to live in Mashpee, and by 1700, the tribe had its own recognized territory. Although many of their traditional beliefs had been suppressed in an attempt to Christianize them, the Wampanoag continued to believe in Moshup.

Struggles

Throughout the eighteenth century, the Wampanoag at Mashpee had their own independent tribal community. However, Massachusetts, first as a colony and then as a commonwealth, frequently intervened in their affairs. In 1788, the Commonwealth of Massachusetts placed the Wampanoag under its control. Declaring the settlement to be a plantation, Massachusetts appointed overseers to help in managing the community, and alternately protected Wampanoag lands and defended its own illegal seizures of tribal territory. In 1833, the Wampanoag rebelled against these intrusions on their land, especially the taking of wood. Led by Native minister "Blind Joe" Amos, Isaac Coombs, Ezra Attaquin, and William Apes, a **Pequot** minister, the Mashpee Wampanoag overthrew the Anglo minister, took control of their meetinghouse, and forbid the cutting of trees on their land. However, they were soon overwhelmed. Apes and the other leaders were imprisoned but released after order was reestablished. The Massachusetts legislature responded in 1834 by changing the status of Mashpee from "plantation" to a district for Native peoples. Mashpee was to be governed as a town, but tribal ownership and control of land was recognized, an arrangement that lasted for twenty-seven years. However, in 1870, the legislature devastated the tribe by dividing most of its land into individual parcels. Then, in 1850, the Herring Pond Reservation near Mashpee was allotted. The Mashpee Wampanoag still managed their town government but lost much of their land.

The Mashpee Wampanoag worked as day laborers, domestic servants, farmers, whalers, soldiers, and basket makers. Around 1840, a Wampanoag named Solomon Attaquin established a popular vacation resort that was visited by writer Henry David Thoreau and statesman Daniel Webster. The resort thrived until 1954, when it was destroyed in a fire. Over the years, several small Wampanoag communities died out or merged with others, yet the Wampanoag strived to preserve and continue traditional beliefs and ceremonies.

In 1602, about three thousand Wampanoag lived on Martha's Vineyard. In 1641, Thomas Mayhew purchased Martha's Vineyard, Nantucket, and the Elizabeth Islands from the British. The newcomers brought European diseases for which the Wampanoag had little or no resistance. By 1674, there were only around 1,200 Wampanoag left on Martha's Vineyard. The people on the three reservations on the island—Chappaquiddick, Christiantown, and Gay Head—were also forced to adapt to a society that nearly destroyed their traditional way of life. In 1870, the principal Wampanoag community on the island, centered at Aquinnah (Gay Head), was granted town status by the Commonwealth of Massachusetts. By 1900, of the three Wampanoag groups on the island, only the one at Aquinnah, the Wampanoag Tribe of Aquinnah (Gay Head), remained. Today, they remain one of two federally recognized Wampanoag tribes in the United States. Never governed by non-Natives, the Wampanoag Tribe of Gay Head has done much to preserve their heritage and assert their contemporary rights.

Language of the Wampanoag

The Wampanoag spoke the Massachusett language, one of five Algonquian languages spoken in southern New England. The other languages were Loup, Narragansett, Mohegan-Pequot-Montauk, and Quiripi-Unquachog. Each of these languages was so similar that speakers of the different languages could usually understand each other. What is known of the Massachusett language comes largely from John Eliot's 1663 translation of the Bible into that language. Today, the language survives in place names, such as Aquinnah; **Hyannis** from Iyanough, meaning "warrior's place;" and Mashpee, meaning "great pond." The first syllables of the names Massachusetts, meaning "big hill;" Mississippi, meaning "big river;" and Massasoit, meaning "big or great chief," are drawn from the Algonquian *massa*.

Although the language of the Wampanoag has been without Native speakers for over 130 years, efforts to preserve the language were taken prior to the language's dying out. Missionaries in the 1600s and 1700s wrote down numerous words and sayings. In the early 2000s, linguists teamed with Wampanoag members to piece through the information available to understand the language and learn it once again. Today, the Wampanoag language is starting to be spoken again at home and in schools on Wampanoag reservations. Following is a sampling of words from *One of the Keys*, compiled and written by Milton A. Travers in 1975, that offers a sense of the people, places, objects, and values important to the Wampanoag.

John Eliot tried to preserve the Wampanoag language by translating the Bible into Massachusett.

The People and Culture of the Wampanoag

Nature

mashtuxet	clear water, as in a brook or pool
mattauquas	cloud
neechipog	dew
ohbee	earth
wekineauquat	fair weather
taquattin	frost
missittopu	great frost
mishaupen	great wind
keesaqushin	high tide
kausitteks	hot weather
capat	ice
wequai	light
cutshausha	lightning
wequashim	moonlight
nittauke nissawanawkamuck	my land (this is my land)
nips	pond
sokenun	rain
mishitashin	storm
nippawus	sun
neimpauog	thunder
mihtuck-quash	tree, or trees
waupi or waban	wind

Places/Travel

kunnosnep	to anchor or tie up a boat
aquetnet	by an island
accomac	beyond the water
aucup	cove
nawwatick	far out to sea

mattapan	good place to set camp
naskeag	good places for shellfishing
micuckaskeete	meadow
chicka, sachimmaacommock	names for a sachem's house
ahtuck	orchard
natick	place in the hills
seip	river
wechekum	sea
acawmuck	to go by water
otan-nash	village, or villages
weta	woods

Objects

anauchemineash	acorns
munnote-tash	basket, or baskets
wampum	beads made from quahog shells
ewachim-neash	corn
causkashunck	buckskin
mishoon	dugout
aumanep	fishing line
machequoce	girdle of wampum
chichegin	hatchet
anawsuck	shells (from shellfish)
mocussinass or mockussinchass	soft leather shoes

Animals

sukkissuog-quahog	clams
anum	dog

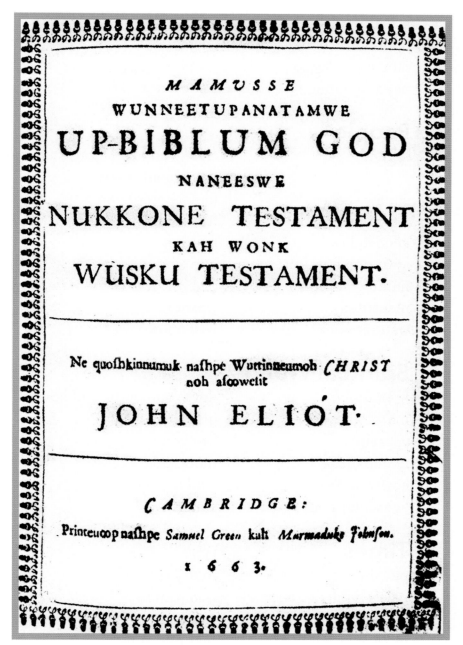

This is a page from John Eliot's bible.

quaquecum-mauog	ducks
ashaunt	lobster
opponenauhock	oysters
tatackommauog	porpoise
neyhome-mauog	turkey, or turkeys

People

sachem	chief who ruled more than one Wampanoag tribe
squaw sachem	female chief
netop-pauog	friend, or friends
keegsquaw	maiden
awaun-nakommit	one who makes a feast
natouwompitea	one who makes the wampum
mecautea	warrior
wauontakick	wise men

Spiritual World

hobomoko	devil, one of the evil spirits
manitou	god
yotaanit	fire god
nanepaushat	moon god
cowwewonck	soul or spirit
keesuckquant	sun god

Times

pausinnummin	to dry corn
paweshaquaw	noontime
aquene	peace
aukeeteaumitch	planting time
paspisha	sunrise

| hawkswawney | time of leisure and storytelling |
| awepu | truce |

While the Wampanoag have endured much since the first encounters with Europeans, they remain today as part of Native American history. They are a modern example of perseverance in the face of adversity. They continue to celebrate their traditions and have taken steps forward to ensure the preservation and survival of their rich cultural identity.

Today the Mashpee Wampanoag celebrate their ancestors with song and dance.

CHAPTER SIX

Reclaiming our language is one means of repairing the broken circle of cultural loss and pain.

—Jessie "Little Doe" Baird, Wampanoag member

THE NATION'S PRESENCE NOW

The Wampanoag exist in the United States and around the world today. There are two federally recognized tribes, the Mashpee in Cape Cod and the Wampanoag Tribe of Aquinnah; however, other Wampanoag tribes also exist. These include the Wampanoag of Assonet, Herring Pond, Nemasket, and Pokanoket. Each has a written constitution, a chief, and an elected tribal council. There is also a council of chiefs for all the Wampanoag, and the mainland Wampanoag recognize a spiritual leader. Within their communities, the Wampanoag are taking action to ensure their culture and history are preserved and passed down through generations. In addition to everything else being done, there is a focus on educating young tribe members in speaking the traditional language of the Wampanoag people.

The Mashpee Wampanoag Today

In the 1920s, the Mashpee Wampanoag and other Wampanoag in Massachusetts began to reclaim their rights and rebuild their identity as a Native people—a vigorous effort that continues to the present. In 1928, two individuals, Eben Queppish, who had been a performer in Buffalo Bill Cody's Wild West Show, and Nelson Simon, who had attended the Carlisle Indian Industrial School in Pennsylvania, united the Mashpee, Gay Head, and Herring Pond communities as the Wampanoag Nation. After Queppish died in an automobile accident in 1933, the Mashpee Wampanoag divided into factions. By the 1960s, the town of Mashpee, like the rest of Cape Cod, was experiencing a frenzy of development. New housing and shifting populations changed Mashpee's voting patterns, and the Wampanoag lost control of the town government and the marine resources on which many people depended for their livelihood. By 1974, non-Natives had come to control the Mashpee town government. The tribe fought these changes by incorporating and filing a lawsuit under the Trade and Intercourse Act to recover lands taken away in 1870.

The People and Culture of the Wampanoag

This image shows Buffalo Bill's Wild West show, which featured Eben Queppish, one of the founders of the Mashpee Nation.

The case went to federal court, but in 1978, a jury determined that the Mashpee was not a tribe and therefore not entitled to its land claim.

Under Grand Sachem Ellsworth Oakley, or Drifting Goose, the Mashpee Wampanoag were able to add the Assonet and Nemasket groups and reorganize in 1975. However, the tribe was denied federal recognition in 1979. It took several decades of hard work to finally achieve recognized status. In 2007, the Mashpee finally gained federal recognition, and in November 2015, they acquired 151 acres (61 hectares) of land.

That same year, the federal government took land in Mashpee and Tauton, both in Massachusetts, and placed it in a trust, formally making the land once more belong to the Mashpee. Tauton likewise gained 171 acres (69 ha) of land. The tribe continues to flourish in other ways. They have been active members of the Wôpanâak Language Reclamation Project since 1993. This program, which partnered with the Massachusetts Institute of Technology (MIT) in 1996, seeks to familiarize all members of the Wampanoag with their Native language. By reading seventeenth- and eighteenth-century documents written by missionaries and other settlers who interacted with the Wampanoag, the project has been able to reconnect the people with their ancestral tongue. It aims to produce more speakers and teachers of the Wampanoag language. One of the main figureheads of the project is Jessie "Little Doe" Baird, a member of the Wampanoag tribe, who earned a MacArthur Fellowship in 2010 for her work. She has spoken openly about the need for the Wampanoag language to return as a regularly spoken language among the Wampanoag people. Her daughter Mae is the first Native Wampanoag speaker in over 130 years. Baird and the project were the subjects of a PBS documentary, *We Are Still Here*, which aired in 2011. The Language Reclamation Project continues to garner success among the Wampanoag people.

The Mashpee have not only preserved the language of their people. They have likewise built and operated a Mashpee museum, which features artifacts and information about the Wampanoag of generations past. They, along with other bands of Wampanoag, do

Jessie "Little Doe" Baird has spent many years preserving and promoting the language and culture of her people.

what they can to ensure their culture and identity as Native Americans is promoted to the wider international community.

To learn more about the Mashpee, visit their website: mashpeewampanoagtribe.com.

The Wampanoag Tribe of Aquinnah Today

The Wampanoag Tribe at Aquinnah has been a federally recognized tribe since 1987. Since 1993, the township of Gay Head has been known as Aquinnah. This is the original Wampanoag term for the area. The township's name was changed to better respect and acknowledge the Wampanoag living in the community. It continues to have great importance to the Wampanoag people today.

The Wampanoag of Aquinnah enjoy significant sovereignty over much of their land and tribal actions. They own in trust several parcels of land on Martha's Vineyard, totaling about 160 acres (65 ha). However, there are also hardships for the tribe. As of 2015, they were struggling to get approval to build a casino and gaming facility on tribal lands. Having such a facility, proposed to be housed in a disused community center, would increase revenue to the tribe and would follow a trend many other Native American groups

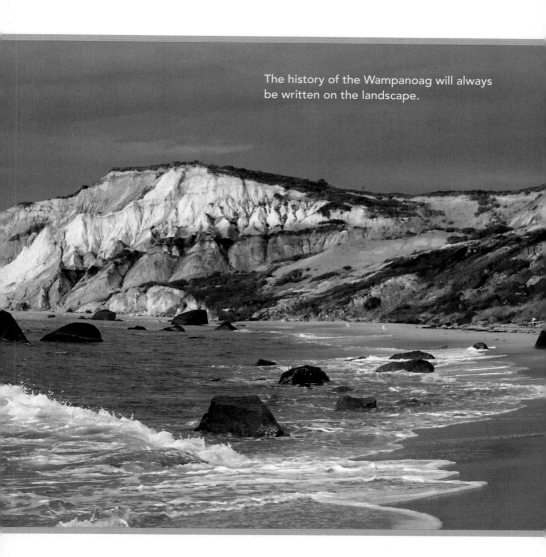

The history of the Wampanoag will always be written on the landscape.

have enacted with success. Despite these efforts, in December 2015, their first proposal was rejected.

The Wampanoag Tribe of Aquinnah has its own government. A tribal council consisting of a chairperson and twelve tribal members makes decisions for the tribe. They are elected by the Aquinnah Wampanoag members, and represent the people in all matters relating to the tribe.

The People and Culture of the Wampanoag

The Wampanoag celebrate their heritage every year with ceremonies, rituals, and dancing.

Tribal facilities include community buildings in which members gather for bimonthly council meetings and general membership meetings, tribal housing, a Wampanoag cultural center, and health care services. In the early 2000s, the Wampanoag of Aquinnah established vigorous cultural, educational, housing, and social service programs. Every summer, they offer a cultural educational program in which participants learn about traditional Wampanoag stories, dances, and music; make items, including pottery and food; and play games. Today, there are over 1,200 enrolled members in the tribe, with about 25 percent residing on Martha's Vineyard. The remaining members live in the United States and around the world.

Every year, the Wampanoag of Aquinnah hold important ceremonies. Two of the most anticipated are the Moshup Pageant in August and Cranberry Day in October. Blending stories, music, and dramatic performances, the Moshup Pageant recalls and honors Moshup's life. Although Cranberry Day once lasted three or four days, this daylong festival is still more significant and meaningful to the Wampanoag than any other holiday. Other ceremonies include powwows, such as the Fourth of July powwow. Members from around the community come to watch this event. To learn more about the Wampanoag of Aquinnah, visit their website: www.wampanoagtribe.net.

Other Tribes

Other bands of the Wampanoag tribe exist. These include the Wampanoag of Herring Pond, Assonet, and Nemasket. These bands are not federally recognized, but they have been significant in promoting Wampanoag traditions, beliefs, and customs. The Assonet and Herring Pond bands are also active participants in the Language Reclamation Project and have put in great effort to help preserve the ways, words, and stories of their people.

Many of the Wampanoag bands are using social media, particularly Facebook, Twitter, and YouTube. To learn more, visit any of the tribes' social media pages. There you will find many tribe-related facts and posts about Native Americans, tribal events and activities, and news about the people who make up the tribe today.

Wherever they live, the Wampanoag are striving to preserve many elements of their culture. They like to believe that Moshup still guides their destiny.

Although the Wampanoag do not have their own schools, they are working to have Native history and culture included in school curricula. Efforts have been made to revive customs such as gathering plants for food and medicine and the traditional arts and crafts.

The Wampanoag have done much to promote their nation and preserve their culture. Their hope is to educate others, as well as people within their own communities, about the traditions and celebrations of their ancestors. Through education, they hope to ensure the tribes' survival for years to come.

Amos Haskins was
a Wampanoag
whaling captain.

*One's sense of identity
is based on family
relations, extended
family, and community.*

—Helen Manning,
Wampanoag of
Aquinnah Elder

FACES
OF THE
WAMPANOAG

There have been many men and women whose actions have influenced the Wampanoag's history. These people belonged to the tribe and helped make the Wampanoag what they are today.

Alexander (Wamsutta) (died 1662), leader, was given his English name after Alexander of ancient Macedonia, on his own request by the court of Plymouth. The son of Massasoit and brother of Philip, he was first in succession as grand sachem when his father died in 1661. Like his father, he sought to continue peaceful relations with the colonists. However, Plymouth leaders, suspecting a Wampanoag and Narragansett conspiracy, summoned Alexander to a hearing. He refused to come and a group of ten colonists, led by Josiah Winslow, went in search of him. They found him feasting in a hunting lodge with his men near present-day Halifax, Massachusetts. Accompanied by his warriors and some of the women, including his wife Weetamo, Alexander was forced to come to Plymouth for a trial. On the way, he became ill with a high fever, and the Wampanoag were allowed to take him home. Alexander died on the return journey. Weetamo suspected that the colonists had poisoned her husband. The death of Alexander was followed by heightened tensions between the Wampanoag and the colonists.

Annawan (Annawon, Anawon) (died 1676), war leader, distinguished himself under Massasoit as *missinnege* of the pnieses, or head of the war leaders. He also served as Philip's principal counselor and strategist. When Philip was killed in August 1676, Annawan took command of the Wampanoag warriors and attacked the colonial settlements of Swansea and Plymouth. Moving camp every night, he eluded Colonel Benjamin Church and his men until an informer helped the colonists locate Annawan in a swamp along the Rehoboth

River on August 26, 1676. At the site now known as Annawan's Rock, the colonists were able to seize most of the warriors' weapons and convince Annawan to surrender. He turned over his tribe's medicine bundle, a deerskin wrapped around a large wampum belt detailing the Wampanoag's history, a small wampum belt representing the confederacy, two powder horns, and a red blanket that had belonged to Philip. The relinquishment of these objects symbolized the end of the war. The prisoners were taken to Plymouth for a trial. Colonial authorities in Plymouth ordered Annawan to be executed. Church, who had come to respect the great leader, argued that Annawan should be spared. However, while Church was away, an angry mob seized Annawan and beheaded him. With the death of the war leader, the Wampanoag Confederacy ended.

Awashonks (active 1670s), sachem, became the leader of the Sakonnet tribe, in the area of present-day Little Compton, Rhode Island, after her husband died. Her tribe was a member of the Wampanoag Confederacy, and during King Philip's War (1675–1676), she permitted some of her warriors to take part in the revolt. After meeting with Colonel Church, she switched sides and supported the colonists. Some of her warriors, including her son Peter Awashonks, then fought against the Wampanoag who had been their allies.

Jessie "Little Doe" Baird (1963–), linguist and educator, is a cofounder of the Wôpanâak Language Reclamation Project. She has spent much of her adult life working toward preserving the language and culture of the Wampanoag tribe, of which she is a member. She received her master's degree in linguistics from the Massachusetts Institute of Technology in 2000 and was awarded a MacArthur Fellowship in 2010. Since 1993, she has worked as the director of the Wôpanâak Language Reclamation Project in Mashpee, Massachusetts. She has inspired many Wampanoag people to learn the language of their people.

Corbitant (Conbitant, Caunbitant) (active 1620s), sachem, possibly the father of Weetamo, was the leader of the Pocasset and Mattapoisett bands, which lived in the area of present-day Tiverton, Rhode Island, and Fall River, Massachusetts. When Grand Sachem Massasoit signed the Treaty of Amity at Plymouth on September 13, 1621, Corbitant argued for resistance against the Europeans, whom he considered to be invaders. He tried to establish a military alliance with the Narragansett and other tribes to drive the colonists back into the sea. He also plotted against Squanto and Hobomok, seizing the two friends of the colonists when colonial leader Miles Standish was away. Hobomok managed to escape and lead Standish and his men to the scene of the attack. After a show of force by the soldiers under Standish, Corbitant accepted a treaty with the colonists.

Hobomok (Hobomoko, Hobbamock) (active 1620–1642), one of Massasoit's councilors, was sent as a special envoy to assist the Pilgrims after they landed at Plymouth in 1620. Along with Squanto, he provided food and showed the colonists how to live in the wilderness, helping them to survive their first hard winter in North America. He served as a liaison between Massasoit and the colonists and as a military advisor to Miles Standish. In August 1621, Hobomok and Squanto were attacked by warriors under Corbitant but managed to escape and inform Standish, who quelled the insurrection. Hobomok converted to Christianity and lived among the colonists at Plymouth until his death in 1642.

This statue shows Iyanough.

Iyanough (Iyannos, Yannis, Jannos) (died 1623), tribal leader, headed the Mattakeeset band, which lived on Cape Cod near present-day Barnstable and Hyannis Port, Massachusetts. A sub-sachem under Grand Sachem Massasoit, he helped the Pilgrims during their first years at Plymouth Colony. With Aspinet, head sachem of the Nauset, he rescued a Pilgrim boy named John Billington, who had become lost in the woods, and returned him to his parents. In the spring of 1623, Massasoit warned the colonists that Iyanough and Aspinet and leaders of the Massachusett and Narragansett were plotting against them. Miles Standish responded by attacking the hostile warriors and driving them into the swamps. While in hiding, both Iyanough and Aspinet died, apparently from diseases they had caught from the colonists.

Helen Manning was an elder of the Aquinnah Wampanoag community.

Helen Manning (1919–2008), elder, was born in Aquinnah (then called Gay Head) in September 1919. She was the daughter of Evelyn Margretta Moss and Arthur Herbert Vanderhoop. She was educated in Washington, DC, and graduated from Paul Laurence Dunbar High School in 1936. During World War II she worked for the War Labor Board. Eventually, she became assistant dean of women at Fisk University

The People and Culture of the Wampanoag

in Tennessee and married her first husband, John Murray. After divorcing Murray following the Korean War, Manning went back to school to get her teacher's license. She took a teaching position in her hometown of Gay Head in 1956. There she met and married her second husband, James Manning, a member of the Wampanoag Tribe. She worked tirelessly as an educator and helped the Wampanoag Tribe of Aquinnah gain its federal recognition in 1987. Eventually, she became involved in the tribal community, being elected to their council board and eventually being considered an elder of the community. One of her lasting contributions to the tribe is a project in which she interviewed and recorded elder members of the Wampanoag community, preserving their stories and traditions for later generations. She died in 2008 at the age of eighty-eight.

Massasoit (Woosamequin, Wasamegin, Osamekin, Yellow Feather) (1580–1661), grand sachem of the Wampanoag in the 1600s, wielded considerable influence over several Native groups from Narragansett Bay to Cape Cod. He encouraged peaceful relations with the English colonists, and often negotiated agreements with the settlers. As early as 1621, with the help of Squanto, who spoke English, Massasoit established friendly trading relationships with the Pilgrims at Plymouth Colony. He traded food in exchange for tools, firearms, and other European goods.

Massasoit offered advice on farming and hunting and gave land to the colonists. He also recommended ways that the Puritan colonists could defend themselves against other tribes. In 1623, he warned them of an impending attack by hostile warriors. Massasoit's alliance with the colonists triggered hostility from those tribes that opposed the English colonists, and the Wampanoag often had to fight these tribes.

The great leader became friends with Roger Williams, a prominent theologian and leader. It is believed that Massasoit influenced Williams's views about the rights of Native Americans. When Williams was accused of heresy and threatened with imprisonment by the Massachusetts colonial government, he fled to Massasoit's home for protection. Despite the efforts of Williams to keep peace, Massasoit came to resent the incessant demands of the English colonists for more land. However, it was Massasoit's son, Philip, who actually went to war with the colonists in 1675.

Although the actual events have been obscured by myths, it is recorded that Massasoit took part in the first Thanksgiving. In 1621, he and several followers came to Plymouth, where they feasted for several days with the Pilgrims. Massasoit and his people supplied five deer for this historic meal.

John Peters (1930–1997), spiritual leader, was born in Hyannis but grew up in the nearby town of Mashpee on Cape Cod. A descendant of the Wampanoag people who first met the Pilgrims, he grew up in a community that strongly maintained traditional beliefs and customs. His family had long been involved in tribal affairs and local politics, with his father serving as a Mashpee selectman for twenty-five years. As a child,

Peters was apprenticed to Billy James, a Mashpee shaman, and he eventually became the spiritual leader for a half dozen Wampanoag groups. In this position, he presided over naming ceremonies, funerals, and other tribal gatherings.

Actively involved in politics, he frequently lobbied on behalf of his people at the Massachusetts State House. He participated in conferences across the nation and lobbied with other Native American leaders on many common interests, including the American Indian Religious Freedom Act of 1978 and the Indian Child Welfare Act of 1978. He also worked on legislation, first in Massachusetts and then in the US Congress, to require the return of skeletal remains to their tribes. Under the federal law, known as the Native American Graves Protection and Repatriation Act, museums and federal agencies must offer to return Native American remains and funerary objects held in their collections.

Philip (King Philip, Metacom, Metacomet) (about 1639–1676), grand sachem, and his brother Wamsutta requested English names from the colonial court and were given the ancient Greek names of Philip and Alexander. He became known as King Philip during the conflict that was named after him. His father Massasoit advocated peaceful relations with the colonists. However, over the years, tension mounted as colonists encroached on Native lands. After Massasoit's death in late 1661, Alexander became grand sachem, but he died the next year, shortly after being summoned to appear before colonial authorities. His widow, Weetamo, who ruled as sachem over the Wampanoag

Pocasset band, suspected that the colonists had poisoned him. Philip probably also suspected foul play when he became grand sachem in 1662 while in his early twenties.

Philip, whose main village was situated at Mount Hope on the west shore of Mount Hope Bay near present-day Bristol, Rhode Island, continued friendly relations with the colonists. He even sold large tracts of land to the newcomers into the late 1670s. However, during this time, he was also organizing other tribes and planning an uprising. Hearing rumors of the revolt, colonial officials ordered the Wampanoag to surrender their guns and sign two treaties. Philip agreed to these conditions because he needed more time. Hostilities in King Philip's War began in 1675, when a confederacy of Massachusett, Mohegan, Niantic, and Wampanoag tribes, with support from the Nauset and Sakonnet, attacked the colonists. Led by Colonel Church, the colonists retaliated, destroying the Native villages. Battles continued through the summer and early winter. By the spring of 1676, the rebellion had been crushed, and the colonial soldiers began hunting down small, defiant bands. In May, Philip's wife Wootonekanuske and his young son were captured. Philip was hiding in Bridgewater Swamp, but Church located him and attacked at dawn on August 12, 1676. In the ensuing battle, Philip was shot and killed.

Squanto (Tisquantum) (circa 1580–1622), ally of the Pilgrims, was a member of the Patuxet band that lived on Cape Cod. It is believed that Squanto was kidnapped in 1614 and taken to Spain with other

The People and Culture of the Wampanoag

Squanto is remembered in artwork around the United States.

Native people and sold into slavery by an English trader named Captain Thomas Hunt. He may have been ransomed by a sympathetic Englishman and taken to England. In 1618 or 1619, he returned to his homeland with Captain Thomas Dermer. He was the only one of the Patuxet captives who had survived the Great Dying, a time ravaged by an epidemic, most likely of smallpox, which had broken out in 1616 and raged for three years.

Somoset, an Abenaki living with the Wampanoag, introduced Squanto to Massasoit and the Pilgrims in March 1621. The grand sachem employed Squanto as an envoy and interpreter to the Pilgrims and helped them to survive their early years at Plymouth Colony. Along with Massasoit, Squanto helped to bring about the first Thanksgiving feast in the fall of 1621. He was also involved in hostilities between the Pilgrims and Native peoples, notably when Corbitant, who was plotting against the colonists, tried to kidnap him. Squanto was able to escape and warn the colonists of the plot against them.

In the autumn of 1622, Squanto agreed to accompany the Pilgrims as guide and interpreter on a trading mission for food with the Narragansett. Heavy seas forced their ship Swan to seek shelter in Chatham Harbor along Cape Cod. Squanto arranged for trade with the local people there. He contracted a fever, probably smallpox, and died at Chatham Harbor.

Weetamo (Wetamoo) (1638–1676), sachem, was born near what is now Tiverton, Rhode Island, and became one of the leaders in King Philip's War. After the death of her first husband, she married Alexander (Wamsutta), who succeeded Massasoit as grand sachem. When Alexander died in 1662, probably from an illness, Weetamo suspected that he had been poisoned.

As sachem of the Pocasset band in King Philip's War (1675–1676), she led attacks on the English colonists. During the Great Swamp Fight of December 1675 in southern Rhode Island, she helped her warriors elude capture. On August 6, 1676, English forces made a surprise attack on her camp in Massachusetts, and she fled down the Taunton River by canoe. The soldiers fired on her, sinking the canoe, and she drowned in the swift current. Her body was later found floating in the Taunton River. The colonists chopped off her head and stuck it on a pole as a gruesome warning to other hostile warriors. Many Native Americans now revere Weetamo as a clever and courageous leader.

These people have inspired many generations of Wampanoag and have enabled the nation to continue today. Without them, the Wampanoag tribe would be very different, and perhaps would not exist. It is efforts by these people and many others that have perpetuated the Wampanoag communities, culture, and customs.

CHRONOLOGY

1602 Bartholomew Gosnold explores Vineyard Sound, the Elizabeth Islands, and Buzzards Bay. An unsuccessful attempt is made to establish a trading post on Cuttyhunk Island in Wampanoag territory.

1603 Martin Pring explores lower Cape Cod. He trades with the Native people but also antagonizes them with large dogs called mastiffs.

1605–1606 Samuel de Champlain leads French expeditions as far south as Cape Cod to explore and trade with the Native people.

1616–1619 Known as the Great Dying, this major epidemic of European diseases reaches Wampanoag villages and devastates the population.

1620 The Wampanoag meet the Pilgrims, who have just arrived in New England.

1621 Grand Sachem Massasoit signs the Treaty of Amity with the Pilgrims.

1628 Massachusetts Bay Colony is established with a large number of settlers.

1631 A smallpox epidemic sweeps through Massachusetts Bay area.

1633 Another smallpox epidemic spreads from New England into southern Ontario.

1636 Roger Williams is expelled from the Massachusetts Bay Colony and flees to what is now Providence, Rhode Island, in territory fought over by the Wampanoag and Narragansett.

1639 Massasoit and his son Metacom (Philip) reaffirm their agreement with Plymouth Colony not to cause any unjust war or sell any land without consent of the colony.

1650 John Eliot founds the first "praying Indian" mission at Natick under the authority of the Massachusetts Bay Colony.

1661 Massasoit dies.

1663 John Eliot publishes the Bible in the Massachusett language.

1671 After being accused of conspiracy, Philip is forced to submit to colonial authority.

1675–1676 King Philip's War leads to the slaughter and enslavement of most Wampanoag people.

1676 Philip is killed in an ambush at Montaup.

1833–1834 Mashpee Revolt leads to limited self-government for the Wampanoag living at Mashpee.

1928 Three Wampanoag groups in Massachusetts unify as the Wampanoag Nation.

1987 Gay Head Wampanoag receive federal recognition.

1993 Wôpanâak Language Reclamation Project begins; township of Gay Head changes name to Aquinnah.

1996 MIT joins Wôpanâak Language Reclamation Project.

2007 Mashpee Tribe gains federal recognition.

2010 Jessie "Little Doe" Baird receives MacArthur Fellowship for her work on the Wôpanâak Language Reclamation Project.

2011 PBS documentary *We Are Still Here* airs.

2015 Mashpee Tribe gains 151 acres (61 ha) of land and have tracts of land placed in a trust by the federal government. Wampanoag of Aquinnah plan to build casino rejected.

GLOSSARY

Algonquian The most widespread group, or family, of languages spoken in North America. Many Native American tribes speak Algonquian languages, including the Abenaki, Arapaho, Blackfoot, Cheyenne, Delaware, Fox, and Shawnee.

Aquinnah The Wampanoag name for Gay Head, a part of Martha's Vineyard.

bandolier A type of belt drawn diagonally over the chest and shoulder or around the waist.

breechcloth A cloth or skin worn between the legs and around the hips; also breechclout.

buckskin Deer hide softened by a tanning or curing process.

clan Members of a large family group who trace their descent from a common ancestor.

cradleboard A wooden board used to carry a baby.

Hyannis A Cape Cod town named for Iyanough, a Wampanoag chief of the 1600s.

Kiehtan The creator and supreme being believed by the Wampanoag to hold the power of life and death.

King Philip's War A major effort led by Metacom in 1675 and 1676 "to push the English back into the sea," as the Wampanoag faced devastation and loss of land.

Mashpee Major Wampanoag community, meaning "big pond" or "big water." Mashpee Pond is the largest body of freshwater on Cape Cod.

Massachusetts Homeland of the Wampanoag people, meaning "big hill."

Moshup Heroic giant who created Martha's Vineyard and Cape Cod and who cared for the Wampanoag in ancient times.

Narragansett Native American people who lived to the west of the Wampanoag.

Noepe Wampanoag name for the island of Martha's Vineyard.

Pequot Native American people who lived to the east of the Wampanoag.

Pilgrims Small group of English immigrants who came to North America seeking religious and political freedom.

pnieses Honored men, advisors, and bodyguards to a sachem, who also served as war leaders.

Pokanoket Name that neighbors and early English travelers used to describe the Wampanoag.

powwow A Wampanoag religious leader and healer responsible for rituals and ceremonies. Also a social gathering where Native Americans come together for dancing and sharing Native crafts and food.

Puritan A group of Protestant Christians that came to America in the 1600s and 1700s. They had strict religious beliefs.

quahog Derived from the Wampanoag word *paqah,* a bivalve mollusk having a purple color along the inside edge of its shell.

sachem Traditional tribal leader, or chief, responsible for the governance and general welfare of his people.

Wampanoag Meaning "People of the East" or "People of the Dawn," Native American people who live in southeastern Massachusetts and Rhode Island.

wampum Valuable beads made of white or purple quahog shells.

weeto A dome-shaped house covered with bark or mats.

weir An enclosure such as a fence that is built to help catch fish.

BIBLIOGRAPHY

Arenstam, Peter, John Kemp, Catherine O'Neill Grace, Sisse Brimberg, and Plimouth Plantation. *Mayflower 1620: A New Look at a Pilgrim Voyage*. Washington, DC: National Geographic, 2007.

Bruchac, Joseph. *Squanto's Journey: The Story of the First Thanksgiving*. Boston, MA: Houghton Mifflin Harcourt, 2007.

Cunningham, Kevin, and Peter Benoit. *The Wampanoag*. True Books: American Indians. New York: Scholastic, 2011.

Dresser, Thomas. *The Wampanoag Tribe of Martha's Vineyard: Colonization and Recognition*. Charleston, SC: The History Press, 2011.

Fisher, Julie A., and David J. Silverman. *Ninigret, Sachem of the Niantics and Narragansetts: Diplomacy, War, and the Balance of Power in Seventeenth-Century New England and Indian Country*. New York: Cornell University, 2014.

Grace, Catherine O'Neill. *1621: A New Look at Thanksgiving.* Washington, DC: National Geographic, 2004.

Gray, Kathryn N. *John Elliot and the Praying Indians of Massachusetts Bay: Communities and Connections in Puritan New England.* Lewisburg, PA: Bucknell University Press, 2013.

Mandell, Daniel R. *King Philip's War: Colonial Expansion, Native Resistance, and the End of Indian Sovereignty.* Witness to History. Baltimore, MD: John Hopkins University Press, 2010.

Philbrick, Nathaniel. *Mayflower: A Story of Courage, Community, and War.* New York: Penguin Group, 2006.

Riehecky, Janet. *The Wampanoag: The People of the First Light.* American Indian Nations. North Mankato, MN: Capstone Press, 2003.

FURTHER INFORMATION

Want to know more about the Wampanoag? Check out these websites, videos, and organizations.

Websites

Wampanoag Fact Sheet

www.bigorrin.org/wampanoag_kids.htm

This website discusses the history of the Wampanoag people.

The Wampanoag Side of the First Thanksgiving Story

indiancountrytodaymedianetwork.com/2011/11/22/
wampanoag-side-first-thanksgiving-story-64076

Read about the first Thanksgiving story, told from the Wampanoag's point of view.

Wôpanâak Language Reclamation Project

www.wlrp.org

Learn about the Wampanoag's language reclamation project, headed by Jessie "Little Doe" Baird.

Videos

The Messenger Runner

www.youtube.com/watch?v=KBTawl-zTyA

This video describes what it was like for Wampanoag tribes to communicate with each other in the 1600s.

Reviving the Wampanoag Language

www.youtube.com/watch?v=_5H1B1uBKtc

Watch this CBS feature about the efforts taken to revive the Wampanoag language.

***We Are Still Here* Documentary**

www.pbs.org/independentlens/films/we-still-live-here

This video describes the efforts being made today by members of the Wampanoag tribe to restore their ancestral language and their heritage.

Organizations

Mashpee Wampanoag Tribe
483 Great Neck Road South
Mashpee, MA 02649
(508) 477-0208
www.mashpeewampanoagtribe.com

Plimoth Plantation

137 Warren Avenue

Plymouth, MA 02360

(508) 746-1622

www.plimoth.org

Wampanoag Tribe of Aquinnah (Gay Head)

20 Black Brook Road

Aquinnah, MA 02535-1546

(508) 645-9265

www.wampanoagtribe.net

Wampanoag Tribe of Herring Pond

PO Box 27

Buzzards Bay MA 02532

(781) 504-4660

www.herringpondtribe.com

INDEX

Page numbers in **boldface** are illustrations. Entries in **boldface** are glossary terms.

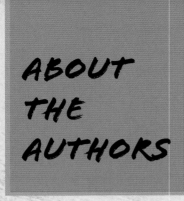

ABOUT THE AUTHORS

Cassie M. Lawton is a freelance editor and writer living and working in New York City.

Raymond Bial has published more than eighty books— most of them photography books—during his career. His photo-essays for children include *Corn Belt Harvest, Amish Home, Frontier Home, Shaker Home, The Underground Railroad, Portrait of a Farm Family, With Needle and Thread: A Book About Quilts, Mist Over the Mountains: Appalachia and Its People, Cajun Home,* **and** *Where Lincoln Walked.*

As with his other work, Bial's deep feeling for his subjects is evident in both the text and illustrations. He travels to tribal cultural centers, photographing homes, artifacts, and surroundings and learning firsthand about the national lifeways of these peoples.

The emeritus director of a small college library in the Midwest, he lives with his wife and three children in Urbana, Illinois.